W9-BFH-401

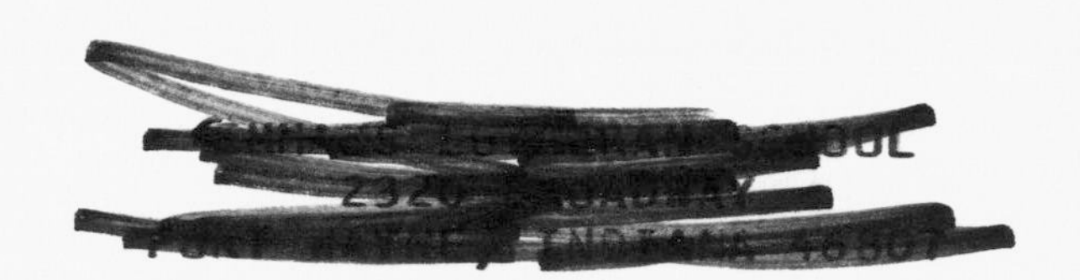

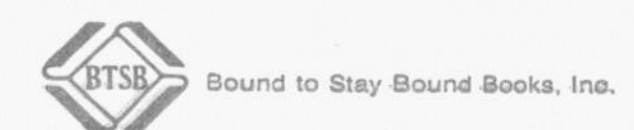
BTSB
Bound to Stay Bound Books, Inc.

FIRST ARTS & CRAFTS

Printing

Sue Stocks

With photographs by Chris Fairclough

Thomson Learning • New York

FIRST ARTS & CRAFTS

Books in this series

Collage
Drawing
Masks
Models
Painting
Printing
Puppets
Toys and Games

For Matilda

First published in the
United States in 1994 by
Thomson Learning
115 Fifth Avenue
New York, NY 10003

First published by Wayland (Publishers) Ltd.

Library of Congress Cataloging-in-Publication Data
Stocks, Sue.
Printing/Sue Stocks; with photographs by Chris Fairclough.
p. cm.—(First arts & crafts)
Includes bibliographical references (p.) and index.
ISBN 1-56847-210-2
1. Handicraft—Juvenile literature. 2. Printing—Juvenile literature. [1. Printing. 2. Handicraft.] I. Fairclough, Chris, ill. II. Title. III. Series: Stocks, Sue. First arts & crafts.
TT160.S76 1994
760'.28—dc20 94-2661

Printed in Italy

Contents

What is printing?

Lots of things are printed. This book is printed. So are newspapers, magazines, and comics. Wallpaper, greetings cards, and fabrics are almost always printed. What other things can you see that have been printed?

You can print in lots of different ways. This book shows you some of those ways. Look at the print below. What do you think it is about?

Copper etching by William Blake (1757-1827) for *The Book of Job*

Get a sheet of paper ready and mix some paint.
Dip the tip of your finger into the paint, then press it onto the paper.
Lift up your finger and press it down again a number of times across the paper until your finger is dry.

Can you see the swirls and whorls in the patterns of your fingerprints?

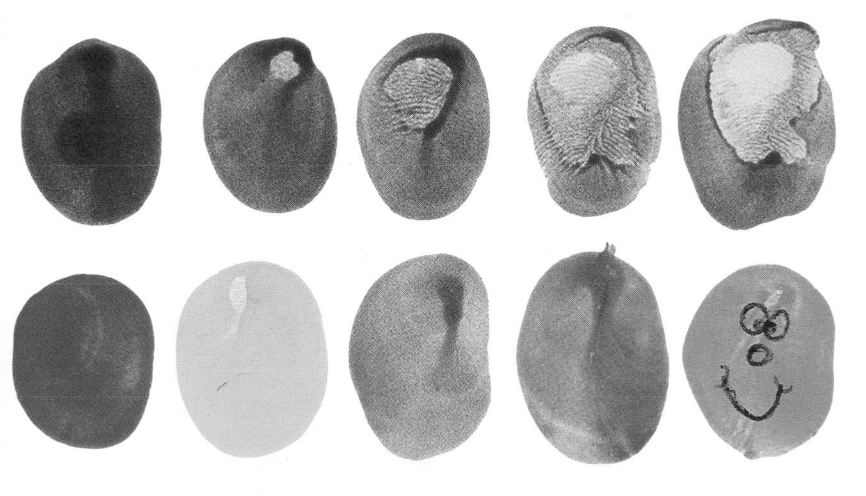

Make more fingerprints using different colors. You can make patterns by printing several fingerprints. You can make a face by drawing hair, ears, eyes, a nose, and a mouth on a fingerprint.

Now make a print with your hand.

Brush paint over your hand then press it onto the paper.

Paint blots

Look at this picture. It is a print made by pressing paper and paint together. You can make your own.

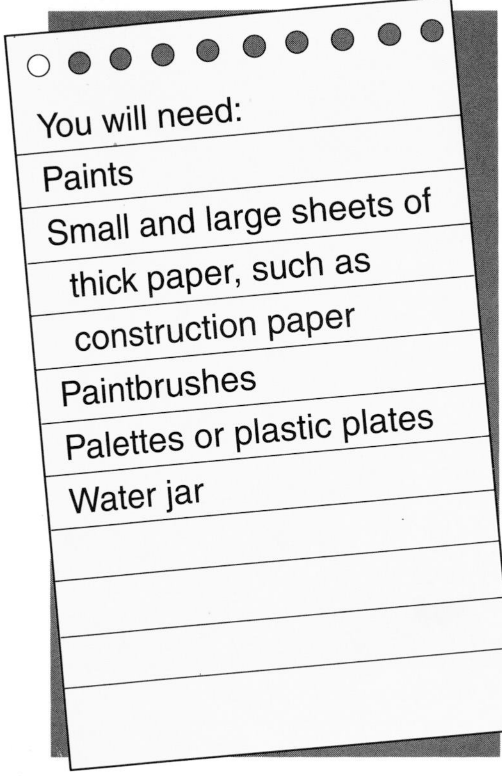

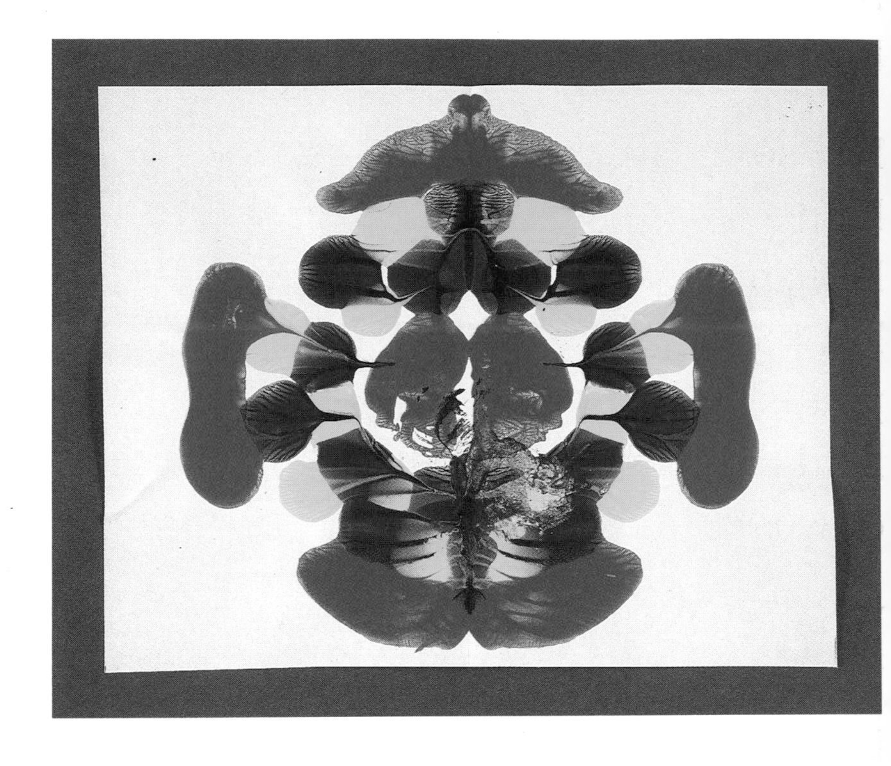

- Mix some paint. Don't make it too watery it should be as thick as cream.
- Fold a small sheet of paper in half, then open it and lay it flat so that you have a piece of paper with a crease down the middle.
- Put a blob of paint on one side of the crease.
- Now fold the other half of the paper over the paint blob. Gently press down with your hand.
- Open the paper again. What do you see?

Make more prints like this using small sheets of paper.

Now you are ready to make a bigger print.

Mix some other paint colors.
Fold a large sheet of paper in half and open it again.
Put blobs of different colored paints on one half of the paper.
Fold the paper over, press down on top, then open it.

What do your paint blots look like? See if you can make some butterfly shapes.

Potato prints

Now you are going to make a potato print
Always ask an adult to help when you are cutting with a knife.

- Cut the potato in half.
- Mix some black paint and have some paper ready.
- Pick up the hairpin at the open end. Press the hairpin into the cut end of half of the potato. Pull it across the top.
  See what happens.
- Wipe the potato dry with a paper towel, then brush some black paint onto the cut end.
- Press it onto the paper. Lift up the potato and see what you have printed.

Make some more cuts in the potato with the hairpin. As you add cuts, make more prints and see what they look like.

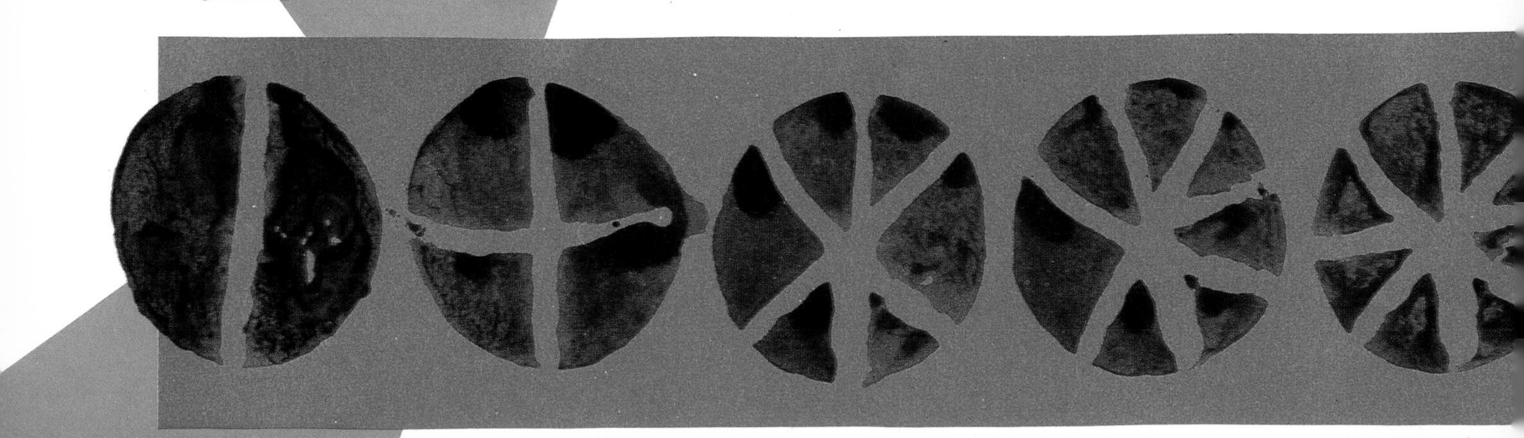

This print is made with lots of small square blocks. Can you see the lines where they join?

You can make more patterns with your potato. When you want to make a new pattern, ask an adult to help you cut off the top of your potato so that you can start again.

Pryde – Pierrot by Eduardo Paolozzi (b.1924). Woodcut.

- Cut pieces from the potato to leave a triangle shape sticking up. Paint it and make a print.
- Now print the triangle upside down.
- Print a line of triangles.

See how many patterns you can make with the triangle print.

Rubbings

Look at this picture. It is another type of print called a rubbing. This one was made in a church. You can make rubbings of almost anything that has a bumpy surface.

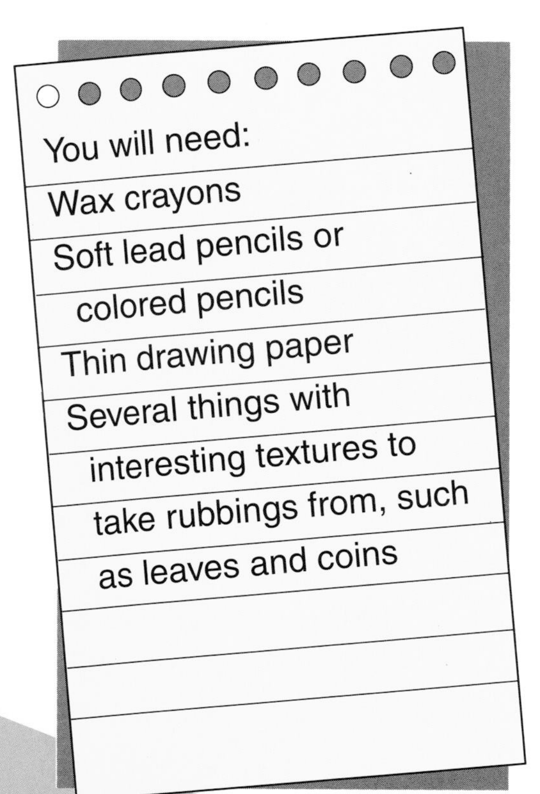

- Put a coin under a piece of paper.
- Rub a wax crayon gently over the top of the paper where the coin is. Hold the paper still over the coin. Rub the crayon smoothly – don't scribble!
  Watch the coin appear.

Look around you. What else can you use to make a rubbing? Collect more things together and make some new rubbings. Go outside and try making rubbings of tree bark, bricks, and wood. There are lots of things you can use.

Collect some leaves.

Make rubbings of the leaves using wax crayons.
Now try pencil and colored pencil. Gently use the side of the lead to make the rubbing.
Fill the paper with rubbings of different shaped leaves.

When you have finished, you will have a sheet of leaves. Put it on the wall. Fill some more sheets of paper with rubbings of leaves and use them as wrapping paper.

Bubble prints

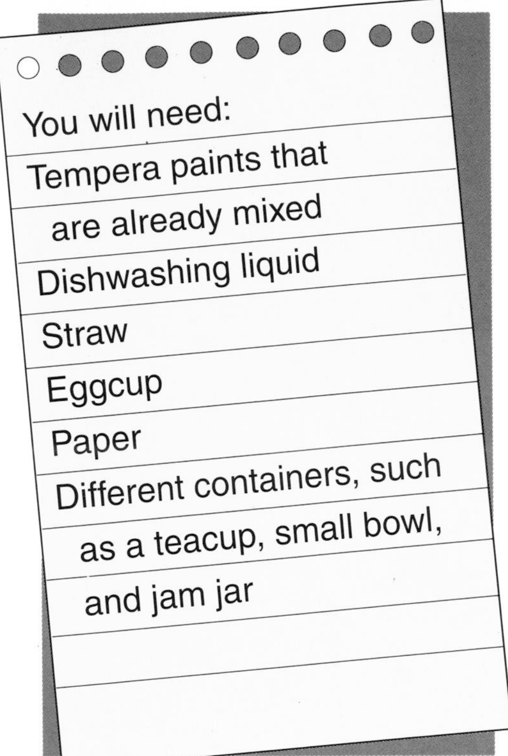

This is another way to make a print. Your prints will get better as you do more of them.

- Have a sheet of paper ready.
- Put some paint in the bottom of the eggcup. Use a bright color.
- Add a squeeze of dishwashing liquid. Mix it gently.
- Put one end of the straw in the mixture. Blow through the straw until the bubbles come to the very top of the eggcup.
- Gently press some paper over the top of the eggcup.

See the bubble print you have made!

Do the same thing with different sized containers. Use a small bowl, a teacup, or a jam jar. Use different colors.

Try adding a second color to your paint mixture.

Put some paint and a squeeze of dishwashing liquid in your container.
Mix it gently.
Add another color to the mixture.
Don't stir it.
Blow bubbles again and lay some paper over the top.

You can make colored patterns using bubble prints. You can print them on cardboard and cut them out to use as gift tags. Make a hole near the edge of the cardboard and push some string or ribbon through.

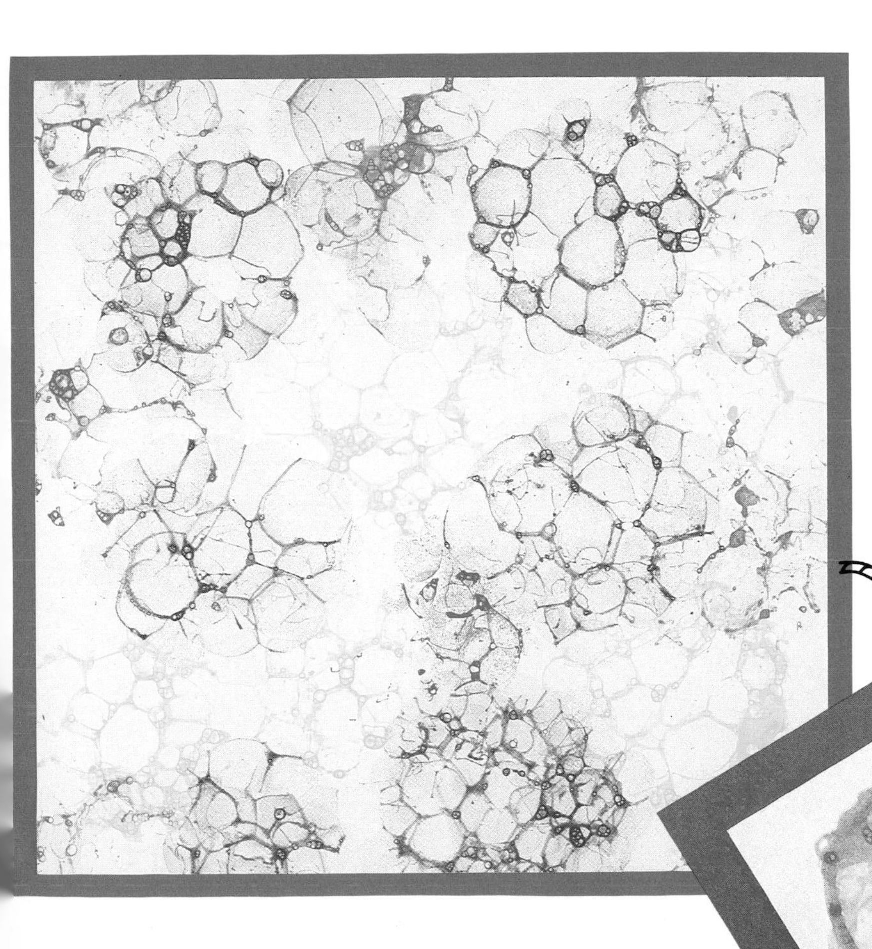

Stenciling

This photograph shows stencil work in the American Museum in Britain, Bath, England. People have decorated their walls and furniture like this for a very long time.

The Stenciled Bedroom (1830) in the American Museum in Britain, Bath, England.

You can use stencils in different ways.

- Cut a simple shape from the middle of a piece of cardboard or stiff paper. Put the cutout shape to one side for use later.
- Mix some paint.
- Lay the cardboard with the shape cut ou over a sheet of paper.

Hold the cardboard still and stencil through the cutout with paint. Try this in different ways:

Use a sponge dipped lightly into the paint – don’t let the sponge get too wet.
Use a stencil brush. Dip the tips of the bristles into the paint, then dab the brush up and down on the cutout.
Dip an old toothbrush into the paint and use a comb to pull back the bristles. Let the paint spatter over the cardboard.

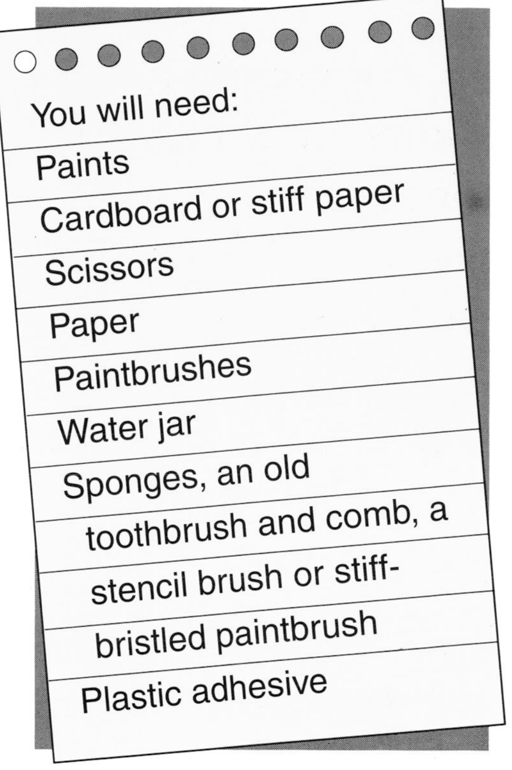

When you have tried all three ways of using your stencil, see how different the finished prints look.

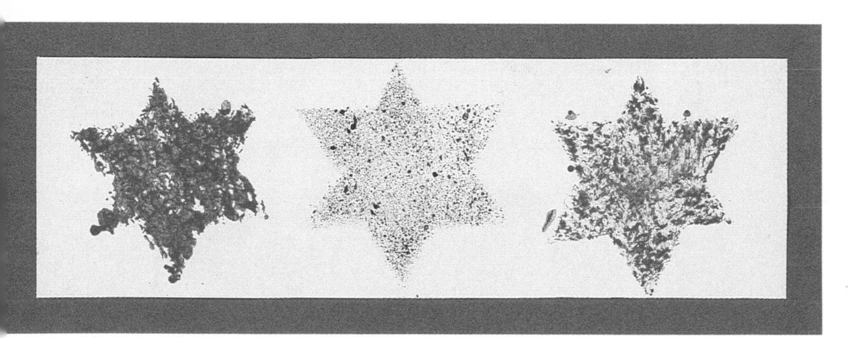

Get the cutout shape you put to the side. Lay it on a sheet of paper. Hold it in place with some plastic adhesive. Paint over the shape using the same three techniques you used before.

Your stencil has made two different kinds of print. The first prints are called positive prints. The second prints are called negative. How are they different?

Fruits and vegetables

Earlier in this book you made prints with a potato. Now make some prints with fruits and other vegetables. This time you don't need to cut out any patterns. Fruits and vegetables cut in half make prints with interesting shapes and textures.

- Mix some paint.
- Brush paint onto the cut side of half an apple.
- Press it down on a sheet of paper.

How do you like the print you have made?

Print a line of apple shapes.
Wash your apple and dry it.
Print more apples using another
color.

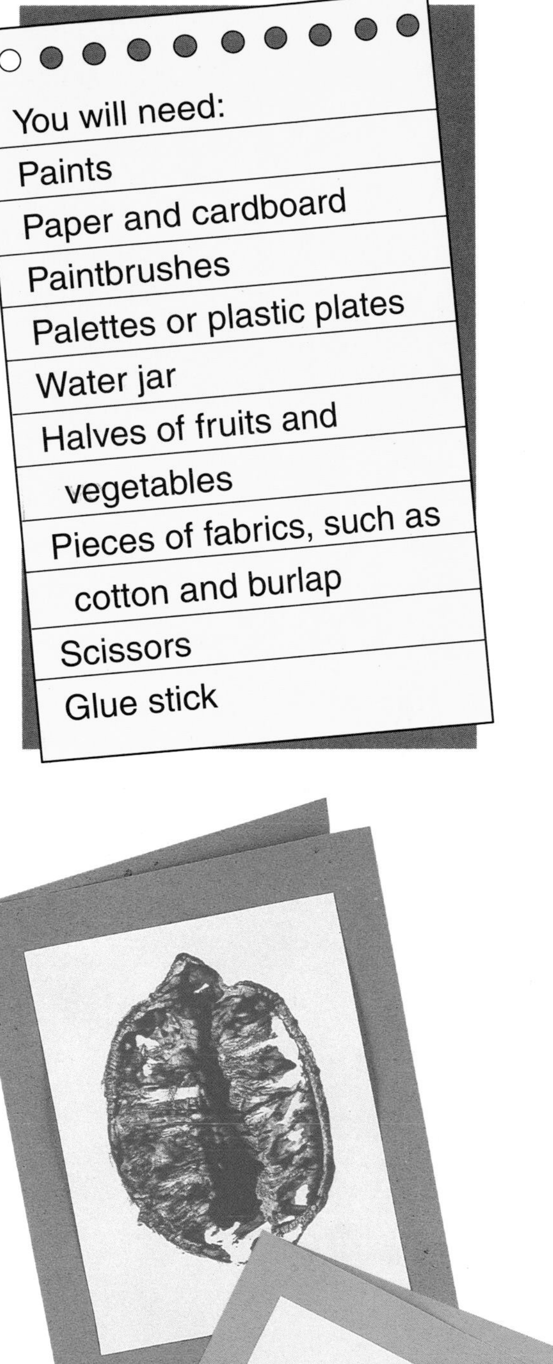

Now try printing with other fruits and vegetables, such as pears or lemons. Print on different types of fabric, such as cotton and burlap. Cut out the best prints and glue them onto small, folded sheets of thick paper. Now you have your own greetings cards.

Print fruits and vegetables on a larger piece of fabric. Make a wall hanging.

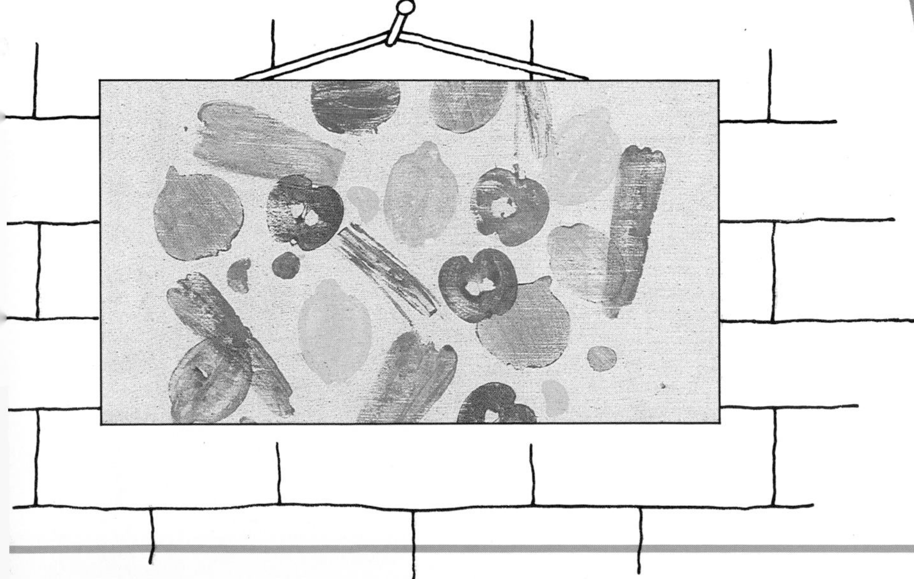

Printing with Styrofoam

You will need:
- Paints (or water-based printing ink with a roller and ceramic tile)
- Paper
- Paintbrushes
- Palettes or plastic plates
- Water jar
- Styrofoam tiles
- Ballpoint pen

Look at this print. The picture tells a story. Look at all the detail in it.

St. Jerome in the Wilderness by Albrecht Dürer (1471-1528)

Make a picture and print it using a Styrofoam tile. First, try something simple.

Use the ballpoint pen to press marks and lines into a Styrofoam tile. Make lots of different marks.
Brush a thick layer of paint across the tile and over your marks.

If you are using ink and a roller, squeeze some ink onto something flat, such as a ceramic tile. Push the roller back and forth across the tile to spread the ink. Make sure the roller is evenly covered with ink. Now push the roller back and forth across the Styrofoam tile two or three times.

Lay a sheet of paper across the top of he paint or ink on the Styrofoam tile. mooth over the paper with your hand. arefully lift the paper off the tile and urn it over to see your print.

lake some more prints like this.

Now you can make a picture on Styrofoam tile. You could draw something in front of you onto the tile. Or you could imagine a picture and draw it. When you have printed your picture, wash the tile, dry it, and make another print using a different color. Print your picture three or four times using other colors.

Relief printing with cardboard

You have made a print by pressing the lines of your drawing into a Styrofoam tile. This time, make a print with pieces of cardboard that are glued onto the tile or another piece of cardboard. This is called relief printing because the picture sticks out from the surface of the tile.

- Take a Styrofoam tile or a small square of cardboard.
- Cut a shape out of another piece of cardboard and glue it onto the square.
- When the glue is dry, brush paint over the cardboard.
- Press the painted side onto a sheet of paper.

Look at this print. See how the different colors change the way the same print looks.

Soup Cans by Andy Warhol (1928?-1987). Silk screen.

Cut out more squares of cardboard with different shapes glued onto them. Print them on colored paper. Look at the same print on different backgrounds.

Now make a bigger picture to print with.

Draw the outline of your family pet, a flower, or anything you like on cardboard. Cut it out and glue it onto a bigger piece of cardboard or a Styrofoam tile.
Make a print with your cardboard on the left side of your paper. Use a pale color.
Wipe the cardboard with a damp sponge. Don't get it too wet.
When the first print is dry, print your picture again with another color. Make it overlap part of the first print. This is called overprinting.
Do the same again with another color.
Make a line of prints across the paper, using pale colors first.

When you have finished, fold your paper like a fan and stand it up.

Relief printing with string

This is a picture of a printing block made from wood. It was used to print patterns on fabric. It could also print on paper.

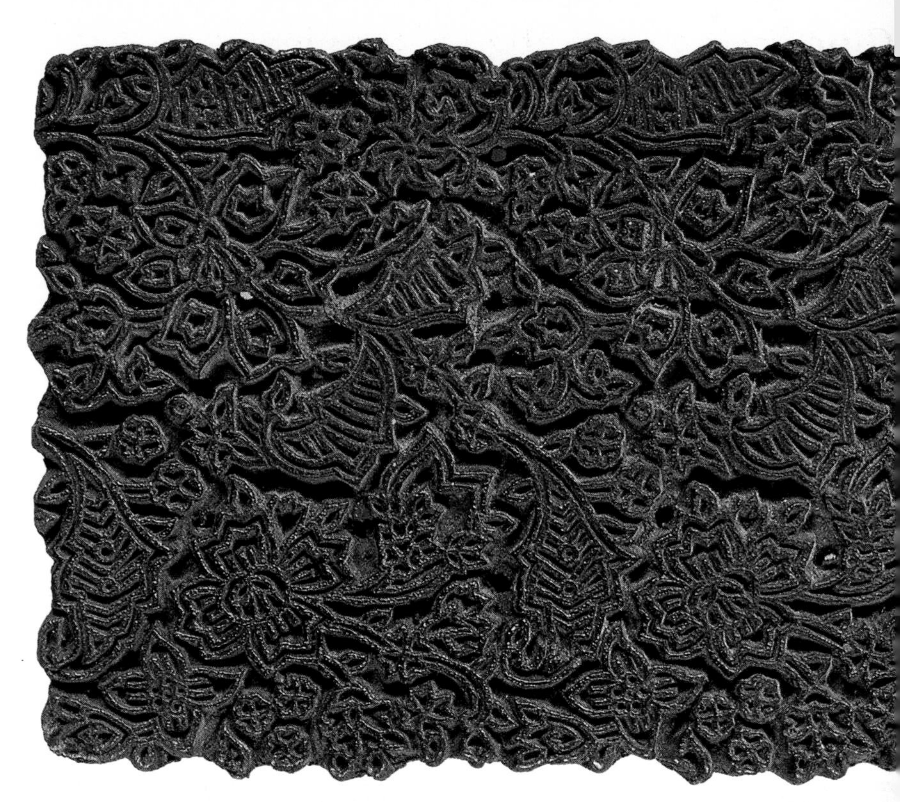

You can make a pattern to print using string.

- Cut out different shapes from cardboard.
- Spread glue on one of the shapes.
- Coil the string on the sticky cardboard. Start at the outside of the cardboard, following the edges of the shape with the string. Fill in the shape as you work towa the middle. Let it dry.
- Do the same with your other shapes.
- When they are dry, roll ink or brush pain over the string shapes and print with them on paper.

Cover a sheet of paper with all your shap in different colors.

Now cut rectangles out of cardboard.
Glue string onto the rectangles in different patterns.
On a large sheet of paper draw a long, swirly snake.
Make prints along the snake's body using your rectangles. Use more than one color. Let your snake dry.
Make a smaller coil of string on a piece of cardboard.
Print the coil along the snake's body over the rectangles. Use a darker or lighter color to make it show up.

Cut out your snake and hang it on the wall.

This black-and-white print is also of a snake. You could make a black-and-white snake, too.

The Serpent 1911 by Raoul Dufy (1877-1953). Woodcut.

Mono-printing

Mono-printing is a different way to print a picture. With mono-printing, you cannot print the same picture again and again as you can with most other prints.

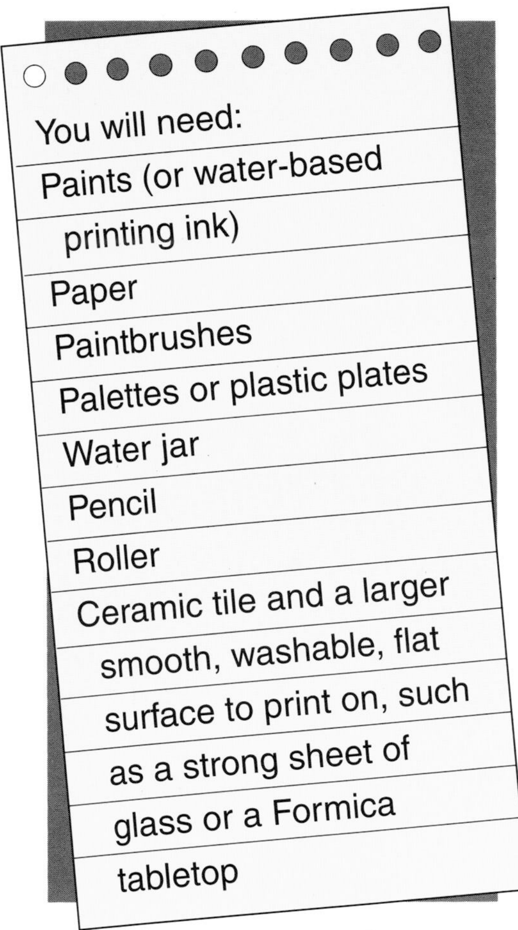

You will need:
Paints (or water-based printing ink)
Paper
Paintbrushes
Palettes or plastic plates
Water jar
Pencil
Roller
Ceramic tile and a larger smooth, washable, flat surface to print on, such as a strong sheet of glass or a Formica tabletop

- Get a piece of paper the same size as the ceramic tile.
- Draw some lines on the paper.
- Mix some paint and brush a thick layer of paint (or ink) onto the ceramic tile.
- Lay the paper, with your drawing facing up, onto the painted tile.
- Using a pencil or the wooden end of a paintbrush, trace over your picture, carefully following the lines. Press firmly. Don't rest your hand on the paper.

Carefully lift the paper up and turn it over. Your picture will be printed on the other side.

Brush more paint or ink over the tile. This time, draw lines into the paint with your finger or the end of your paintbrush. Lay a sheet of paper over the tile. Push a dry roller over the paper.

Lift up the paper and see your new print. Does it look different from the first one?

Now make a bigger picture using a larger printing surface, such as a Formica tabletop. Ask an adult what you can use. Draw a picture of someone in your family. Make some prints using both techniques. Do you like one way more than the other?

Moonshine by Edvard Munch (1863-1944). Woodcut.

This print is called a woodcut. The artist used very sharp tools to cut the picture out of the wood.

Printing with textures

Look at this picture. It was made by printing with different objects.

Collect all the objects you can think of that would make interesting prints. You could try corks, feathers, netting, leaves, sponges, and crumpled paper.

You will need:

- Paints (or water-based printing ink and a roller)
- Paper
- Paintbrushes
- Palettes or plastic plates
- Water jar
- A variety of things to print with, such as crumpled paper, feathers, and leaves
- Strong cardboard
- Different colored paper

- Get a large sheet of paper ready. Mix some paint.
- Try printing in different ways with all the things you have found.

Cover the paper with your prints. Which objects make the best prints?

Glue your objects to a sheet of strong cardboard. Try crumpling fabric and sandpaper as well. All the objects must be the same height so that they will all print together.
Lay a sheet of paper over the objects on the cardboard.
Use the roller to roll paint or ink over the top of the paper. Watch the different textures appear.

Tear some strips from sheets of different colored paper. Glue them onto a large piece of colored paper and print onto this in the same way.

Now brush ink or paint onto the objects on the cardboard. Turn it over and lay the painted side on paper. Press down, then lift it up to see your print.

Weimar Bauhaus Poster by Paul Klee (1879-1940). Lithograph.

The picture above shows a different kind of print. It is a design for a poster. How would you print your own poster?

Windows

This photograph shows a view through a window.

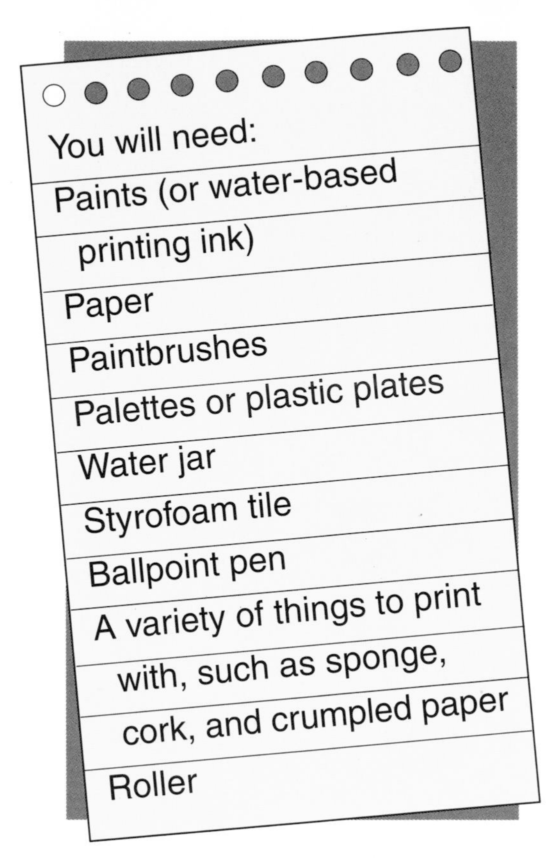

You will need:

- Paints (or water-based printing ink)
- Paper
- Paintbrushes
- Palettes or plastic plates
- Water jar
- Styrofoam tile
- Ballpoint pen
- A variety of things to print with, such as sponge, cork, and crumpled paper
- Roller

Look out a window. What can you see? You can make a print of the view from a window. First, look at the view and think about the things you can use to make a print of what you see. A sponge could make the sky, and small rectangles could make bricks. Scrunched up paper could make leaves on trees.

Collect all the objects you want to print with.
Make lots of prints with your objects on a big sheet of paper. Don't put too much paint on the objects when you print.

See the different patterns and textures your prints have made.

Now draw the view from your window on a Styrofoam tile. Draw only the outlines of things. Use the ballpoint pen to press the lines into the tile.

- Roll paint or ink over your drawing. Choose a pale color.
- Lay a sheet of paper over the tile. Smooth it down with your hand.
- Lift off the paper and turn it over.

When it is dry, over-print your picture with all the things you have chosen. Make your view through the window colorful.

Helpful hints

You can make a print with almost anything on almost anything that will take paint or ink. The more you use your imagination, the better your prints will be. Let the techniques in this book give you ideas for your own techniques. Let prints in museums, pictures in books, and everyday scenes inspire you. Practice making prints, use your imagination, and have fun!

- Make prints of your own hands and feet.
- Brown parcel paper, scrap paper, and even newspaper make good surfaces on which to paint.
- Keep your work area neat. Always spread newspaper or plastic on your work surface. Print in a room with a washable floor, or spread newspaper or plastic on the floor around your work surface.
- Wear old clothes or a smock when you print.
- Corrugated cardboard makes a good printing surface. You can cut it into different shapes.
- Make a huge print by taping paper together.
- Try printing wrapping paper and a matching card.
- Set up a gallery on your bedroom wall. You can put your prints in inexpensive plastic frames, tack them all to a bulletin board, or use plastic adhesive to hang them on the wall.
- Ask a friend to make collages with you.

Glossary

Burlap A strong fabric with a rough surface that is used to make sacks.

Ceramic tile Tiles made of clay that often cover walls and floors in bathrooms, kitchens, and halls.

Crease A line left in paper or fabric that has been folded.

Greetings cards The cards given to people on special days such as birthdays.

Hairpin A flat pin shaped like a "U" that is used for holding hair in place.

Negative print A print in which only the background of a picture or shape is printed. The picture itself is not printed and shows as the color of the paper on which it was printed.

Overlap Laying part of one thing over part of another.

Overprinting Printing over something that has already been printed.

Pattern Shapes and colors that are repeated.

Positive print A print in which the picture or shape itself is printed with paint or ink.

Printing Pressing words or pictures onto a background, such as paper or fabric.

Relief printing Printing with a picture or pattern that sticks out from the tile or piece of cardboard being printed with.

Stencil A piece of cardboard with a pattern cut out of it. The pattern is printed onto the surface beneath by painting through the cutout.

Surface The outside or top of something.

Techniques Ways of doing something. In this book, they are different ways of printing.

Texture The feel or look of a surface.

Further information

Further reading

Amery, H. and Civardi, Anne. *Print & Paint: Lots of Ways to Make Pictures and Patterns.* Tulsa: EDC Publishing, 1977.

O'Reilly, Susie. *Block Printing.* Arts & Crafts. New York: Thomson Learning, 1993.

Stocks, Sue. *Painting.* First Arts & Crafts. New York: Thomson Learning, 1994.

Tofts, Hannah. *The Print Book.* Color Crafts. New York: Simon & Schuster Books for Young Readers, 1990.

Index

Acknowledgments

The publishers wish to thank the following for the use of photographs:
Bridgeman Art Library Ltd. for Pablo Picasso's linocut (front cover) *Bust of Woman, After Cranach the Younger,* © DACS 1994;
Visual Arts Library for Albrecht Dürer's *St. Jerome in the Wilderness*; Andy Warhol's *Soup Cans,* © 1993 The Andy Warhol Foundation for the Visual Arts Inc.; Edvard Munch's *Moonshine,* © Munch Museum/Munch Estate/BONO, OSLO/DACS, London 1994; Raoul Dufy's *The Serpent 1911,* © DACS 1994, and Paul Klee's *Weimar Bauhaus Poster 1993,* © DACS 1994;
Eduardo Paolozzi for *Pryde – Pierrot;*
William Blake's copper etching for *The Book of Job* reproduced by kind permission of Andrew Soloman.
The Stenciled Bedroom, reproduced by kind permission of the American Museum in Britain, Bath ©.

The publishers also wish to thank our models Kerry and Manlai, and our young artists Sue and Rebecca.